The Living Eulogy Journal
A Year of Sharing Gratitude and Becoming Happier

By
Rusty Williams

The Barefoot Ministries

THE LIVING EULOGY JOURNAL:
A Year of Sharing Gratitude and Becoming Happier

Copyright © 2021 by Rusty Williams.

All rights reserved. Printed in the United States of America. No part of this publication may be reproduced, distributed, or transmitted in any form or by any means, including photocopying, recording, or other electronic or mechanical methods, without the prior written permission of the publisher, except in the case of brief quotations embodied in critical reviews and certain other noncommercial uses permitted by copyright law.

ISBN: 978-1-7361579-4-7

First printing edition 2021

The user of this journal does so at their own risk and assumes all responsibility for following the suggestions offered therein. The content of this journal is for information purposes only, and is not intended to diagnose, treat, cure, or prevent any medical or mental health condition. The user of this journal understands that this book is not intended as a substitute for consultation with a licensed practitioner. If you are unsure whether sharing your thoughts and gratitude for others will affect you in any way that is contradictory to anything you might want or anticipate, or to any treatment or therapy you are undergoing, or have been undergoing or diagnosed with in the past, you should consult with a healthcare provider, therapist, or licensed counselor before starting this journal.

Published by The Barefoot Ministries
149 Sitting Bull Trail
Medford Lakes, NJ 08055
www.thebarefootministries.org

The Living Eulogy Journal

A Year of Sharing Gratitude and Becoming Happier

Table of Contents

Section 1

Chapter 1: Expressing Gratitude 1

Chapter 2: Identifying Fifty-Two People Who Influenced Your Life 5

Chapter 3: Using This Journal 9

Section 2

Chapter 4: Sharing Living Eulogies Once a Week 15

    Progress Check 1 25

    Progress Check 2 71

    Progress Check 3 116

Section 3

Chapter 5: Taking It To Another Level 127

    Personal Eulogy 132

    The Eulogy I Never Gave 134

Chapter 6: Closing Thoughts 137

The Living Eulogy Journal

A Year of Sharing Gratitude and Becoming Happier

Section 1

Chapter 1: Expressing Gratitude

In just a few sentences, how would you describe the most important person in your life? How would you describe other influential people in your life? That's right, just a few sentences.

Have you ever told these people how grateful you are for the difference they've made in your life? Sure, we tell those close to us, those who are dear to us, how grateful we are that they are in our life; we might even do that often. But, do we take it to the next level?

The next level would be to tell them why they mean so much to us and why we're grateful for them in our life; to share with them our gratitude while they are still alive to hear it. Unfortunately, most people wait until a funeral or a memorial service to share why someone meant so much to them and what we learned from them. Wouldn't both the giver and the receiver of this information be served better if it was shared while both people were still alive?

What if you were to learn that psychologists have shown that one of the greatest contributing factors to overall happiness in your life is how much gratitude you show? According to a 2013 experiment, participants in a study who shared their gratitude with the person they were appreciative of had between five to ten times higher increase in happiness than participants who simply wrote down their gratitude but didn't share it with that person. In other words, expressing gratitude, not simply feeling it, exponentially increases happiness.

In this same study, the participant who had the greatest increase in their level of happiness was the person who scored the lowest in happiness before the experiment started. So, for someone having a difficult time, sharing gratitude has the potential to increase your happiness by a factor of up to ten times. How's that for some good news on a lousy day?

The experiment is called *An Experiment in Gratitude: The Science of Happiness* (July 11, 2013) and can be found on YouTube and other social video sites. In this video, volunteers were asked to think of someone special in their lives, someone who was important or influenced who they are today. These volunteers where then asked to write down why this person was so special. Most of the participants thought that was the end of the experiment. However, the participants were then handed a phone and asked to call the person they wrote about and read to them what they had written. If you have the time, I highly recommend watching the video.

With this experiment as a foundation, let's consider for a moment that there are a lot of people who have helped us, who have been there for us, who we've enjoyed sharing time with, and maybe who have even saved us from something. Can we both agree that these people exist in the world, and that many of them are still alive? Great!

And, here's where this journal differs from all other gratitude journals. Those journals allow you to write down what you're grateful for – either every day or every week. You write down those things that made you happy, and then you're probably given an opportunity to consider them and think about them. But, you keep them to yourself; you don't share that gratitude with anyone. And, as the experiment in the video shows, you'll be much happier if you're given the opportunity to share your gratitude instead of keeping it to yourself. This journal doesn't just give you the opportunity to share it, it encourages you to share that gratitude.

Now, just like in the video, in a moment you're going to be asked to close your eyes and think of people who mean a lot to you; think of those special people who have influenced you, who have helped you, who are your family or who are like family; think of special teachers, coaches, people in the helping professions; think of neighbors you currently have and neighbors from other places you've lived, think of childhood friends and new friends, coworkers or schoolmates; think of those who made your needs a priority, people who had your best interest at heart, people who went out of their way to make sure you were ok; consider people who gave you a smile when you needed it, a hug, a handshake or even a simple acknowledgement, and those whose simple act of kindness made your day. Is there anyone else? They might be immediate and extended family members, mentors, or even heroes. There is no wrong name in your list; indeed, whatever name first pops in your head is the name it should be.

In the lines on the next two pages, you're going to write down the names of the people who come to mind. Don't worry about putting them in order, don't worry about what to say about them, just write their names on the blank lines. If you run out of names before you get to 52 of them, put this journal down and get on with some task you need to do; get busy doing something other than thinking of names of people. Sometime later, you'll think of a name, or it will pop in your head. When it does, come back and write it down. Repeat this until you have names in all 52 lines.

Remember, you have a year to fill in all 52 lines. You'll undoubtedly meet people in the upcoming 12 months, and some of those people might become important to you. You can add their names to this list as time goes on. And, just as surely, you'll think of names in the weeks and months ahead that aren't coming to your mind right now – and, that's ok. As different people come to mind, write their name in the list and before you know it, you'll have those 52 lines filled with names of people who have meaning in your life.

Ok, it's time. Go ahead and close your eyes and think of those names and write them down… Close your eyes again, and write down more names that come to your mind…

That's right; you've got this!

The Living Eulogy Journal

A Year of Sharing Gratitude and Becoming Happier

Section 1

Chapter 2: Identifying Fifty-Two People Who Influenced Your Life

Names of people who are important to me include:

1. _____
2. _____
3. _____
4. _____
5. _____
6. _____
7. _____
8. _____
9. _____
10. _____
11. _____
12. _____
13. _____
14. _____
15. _____
16. _____
17. _____
18. _____
19. _____
20. _____
21. _____
22. _____
23. _____
24. _____
25. _____
26. _____

_____
_____
_____
_____
_____
_____
_____
_____
_____
_____
_____
_____

27. _____
28. _____
29. _____
30. _____
31. _____
32. _____
33. _____
34. _____
35. _____
36. _____
37. _____
38. _____
39. _____

40. _____
41. _____
42. _____
43. _____
44. _____
45. _____
46. _____
47. _____
48. _____
49. _____
50. _____
51. _____
52. _____

_____
_____
_____
_____
_____
_____
_____
_____
_____
_____
_____
_____

The Living Eulogy Journal

A Year of Sharing Gratitude and Becoming Happier

Section 1

Chapter 3: Using This Journal

Alright, you've got your list; nice job! It's interesting, isn't it, the number of people in our lives who have helped us, who were there for us, who've made a difference or influenced us in some way? Wouldn't you also agree that they deserve to know it? Can you imagine how wonderful they'll feel when they hear they made even a small difference in your life? And, that's not hard to imagine, is it? After all, you can imagine now what that might feel like if you received a call and heard how you made a difference in the life of someone. It would be nice, wouldn't it?

In order to do that, in order to share with someone why they mean so much to us and why we're grateful for them in our lives, we first have to put our thoughts into words so they make sense. After all, if this were that person's memorial service, and we were asked to share a eulogy, we would write down our thoughts and make sure we got everything down that we wanted to say. And, of course, we wouldn't worry about grammar or punctuation – this will be spoken, and all of us talk differently than the way we write. So, don't be concerned about anything other than getting those thoughts down – writing down why this person is important, why you're grateful, or why they mean so much to you. A few words in an outline form work just as well as full sentences separated by paragraphs. Whatever you're most comfortable with is the way you should write it down.

And, whatever way you write it, make sure it is in the present tense; make sure your words convey why you are sharing this with them *now*. For example, if I was writing about me, I would use phrases such as "Rusty goes out of his way to make others around him feel welcome." That statement is in the present tense. Compare that with something you wouldn't write: "Rusty always went out of his way to make others around him feel welcome." Do you see the difference? In the first statement, there is no doubt in anyone's mind that Rusty is still among the living; however, in the second statement, one might think that Rusty is no longer here with us (since the statement talks about the past). And, imagine how the person you're reading it to is going to feel; even if it was the nicest thing anyone ever said about me, I would probably be uncomfortable hearing my name used in the past tense as if that is what I used to do. Make sense?

One more thing to consider is this: How you refer to the person you're reading the eulogy to – the person from your list that you chose for that week's sharing. In the previous paragraph, notice how I used my name in the examples. A living eulogy is a gift to the person receiving it, so there is really no wrong way to deliver it. But, there are some suggestions to make it the most meaningful it can be; the previous paragraph suggested one. One other suggestion is to use the person's name instead of referring to them as "you." Notice the difference between, "*Rusty* is the kind of person who…" and "*You* are the kind of person who…" Something very special happens when we hear our names; and it's even better when we feel like we're listening in on a conversation where we're being talked about in a positive way. So, it is suggested that you use the person's name in the eulogy, just as you would if you were delivering it at their service.

And, just as there was no right order to write down the names, there is no right order in which to choose who you will write about each week. The first name from the list that seems right is the right one to start with. You could start with the first name, but you could start in the middle – or anywhere else on the list. Again, allow yourself to go with whatever feels right. Maybe you want to go oldest to youngest, or youngest to oldest; maybe you want to go with who you've known the longest to shortest, or shortest to longest; or maybe you want to randomly pick a name each week. Again, whichever way you choose is the way it's supposed to be.

In the next section of this journal, you'll start with the person who you are going to write about – the person who you are grateful for. You'll write their name at the top of the first page of each week, then you'll write down three or four of the *how's* and the *why's*: how they've influenced your life, how they've made a difference in it, how their best traits have made you a better person, why they mean so much to you, why they're important, why you describe them to others the way you do, and how you'll always remember them. If you get stuck or aren't quite sure how to begin, you can use the previous sentence as a template:

- How has this person influenced your life?
- How has this person made a difference in your life?

- What traits has this person shared that have made you a better person?
- Why does this person mean so much to you?
- Why is this person important to you?
- How do you describe this person to others?
- How will you always remember them?

You don't need to write a chapter of a book; three or four key moments or examples of why they mean what they mean to you, three or four reasons or memories – just a handful of the how's and why's – is all you need. Different thoughts will certainly come to mind during your talk with this person, so just allow yourself to go with the flow while in conversation with them.

Now that you've written this person's living eulogy, you're going to call them. You could just as easily read this to them in person, but there is something unique that happens when a person receives a phone call. Additionally, there is a sense of safety for you, the reader of the eulogy; the distance a phone call provides keeps it personal, and yet it gives you a safe space to read it.

When you do call this person, you'll have to decide how you want to start the call. There is no right or wrong way to start; whatever way makes you feel the most comfortable is the one that will be the most meaningful, and your approach may vary depending on who you are calling.

You could start by saying, "Hello, _____, I have something to read to you and I want you to let me finish before you comment." Or, "Hello, _____, I want to share with you something I wrote down." You could even say, "Hello, _____, I was thinking about you, and I wrote a eulogy about you just as if I was sharing it if you were to die. Instead of waiting until then, I want to make sure you hear it when you are still alive."

Say whatever words feel natural to you. You might even tell them you are keeping a weekly journal, tell them the name of the journal, and let them know you've selected them for this week's gratitude share. In fact, if you start with this, you'll be framing the rest of the conversation to that of sharing gratitude on a weekly basis.

Once you say your opening line(s), simply read what you have written, just as if you were reading it at a funeral or memorial service. If you get emotional, don't apologize; you are human and human emotions are meant to be shared. If you think you might get emotional, practice reading what you've written a couple of times; this tends to help – at least it does with me. In fact, now that I've seen what I've just written, I'm going to say that it is a good idea to practice reading the eulogy a couple of times before you call each person on your list. After you call each person, and say good-bye, there is a place in each section for you to share your feelings.

Ok, the rest is up to you. Now it's your turn. This is your opportunity to not only experience increased happiness for the next 52 weeks, it's also your opportunity to make someone's day – to even make their year. I promise, it will change your life and the lives of at least 52 other people.

Get going. You've got this!

The Living Eulogy Journal

A Year of Sharing Gratitude and Becoming Happier

Section 2

Chapter 4: Sharing Living Eulogies Once a Week

Use the following pages to write your appreciations for the people on your list. Have fun and be prepared to be surprised, delighted, and deeply grateful.

"When you have a dream, you've got to grab it and never let go."
Carol Burnett

Week 1

The person I'm acknowledging and will call this week is:

_____

I'm grateful for this person who has influenced me, and is important to me, because:

_____
_____
_____
_____
_____
_____
_____
_____
_____
_____
_____
_____
_____
_____
_____
_____
_____
_____

Reactions:

The reaction of _____ was:
(person you called)

_____
_____
_____
_____

I had the following thoughts, feelings, and emotions just before reaching this person:

_____
_____

I had the following thoughts, feelings, and emotions while I was reading the eulogy:

_____
_____
_____
_____

After saying good-bye, I have the following thoughts, feelings, and emotions:

_____
_____
_____
_____
_____
_____

"The bad news is time flies. The good news is you're the pilot."
Michael Altshuler

Week 2

The person I'm acknowledging and will call this week is:

_____

I'm grateful for this person who has influenced me, and is important to me, because:

_____
_____
_____
_____
_____
_____
_____
_____
_____
_____
_____
_____
_____
_____
_____
_____
_____
_____
_____

Reactions:

The reaction of _____ was:
(person you called)

_____
_____
_____
_____

I had the following thoughts, feelings, and emotions just before reaching this person:

_____
_____

I had the following thoughts, feelings, and emotions while I was reading the eulogy:

_____
_____
_____
_____

After saying good-bye, I have the following thoughts, feelings, and emotions:

_____
_____
_____
_____
_____
_____

"Yesterday is not ours to recover, but tomorrow is ours to win or lose."
Lyndon B. Johnson

Week 3

The person I'm acknowledging and will call this week is:

_____

I'm grateful for this person who has influenced me, and is important to me, because:

_____
_____
_____
_____
_____
_____
_____
_____
_____
_____
_____
_____
_____
_____
_____
_____
_____

Reactions:

The reaction of _____ was:
(person you called)

_____
_____
_____
_____

I had the following thoughts, feelings, and emotions just before reaching this person:

_____
_____

I had the following thoughts, feelings, and emotions while I was reading the eulogy:

_____
_____
_____
_____

After saying good-bye, I have the following thoughts, feelings, and emotions:

_____
_____
_____
_____
_____

"Success is not final, failure is not fatal: it is the courage to continue that counts."
Winston Churchill

Week 4

The person I'm acknowledging and will call this week is:

_____

I'm grateful for this person who has influenced me, and is important to me, because:

_____
_____
_____
_____
_____
_____
_____
_____
_____
_____
_____
_____
_____
_____
_____
_____
_____
_____
_____

Reactions:

The reaction of _____ was:
                    (person you called)

_____
_____
_____
_____

I had the following thoughts, feelings, and emotions just before reaching this person:

_____
_____

I had the following thoughts, feelings, and emotions while I was reading the eulogy:

_____
_____
_____
_____

After saying good-bye, I have the following thoughts, feelings, and emotions:

_____
_____
_____
_____
_____

Progress Check 1

Progress check: How are you doing so far? It's been a month since you started and that means you've shared four living eulogies. It means you've positively influenced the lives of four people; four people who, before you shared your gratitude, weren't aware of the difference they've made in your life. By sharing your gratitude with them, these four people experienced gratitude of their own. And, I bet it made a difference in their life; at the very least, you made their day.

And, after your call to each of them, you have to wonder the effect their gratitude had on others. Think about it, your call triggered something in them, and whatever was triggered, it positively changed their attitude for the better. And, if they had a different, more positive, outlook on life, they more than likely treated other people in their lives in a positive way. Maybe they were feeling so good about the call you made that after it, they waved to a neighbor, or remembered to use all five fingers when they waived to the driver of a car trying to merge in front of them. And then those people felt better about their day, and maybe they did a small act of kindness for a stranger.

Your short phone call was the first domino in a chain-reaction of kindness and gratitude. And, by calling these first four people, that chain-reaction has now quadrupled. Gratitude was quadrupled. Kindness was quadrupled. And, in that process, the influence you had on humanity was multiplied by a factor of four.

Knowing this, how do you feel about the difference you've made in people's lives? Did it get easier to call each person as each week went by? How much are you looking forward to calling the other people on your list?

By now, you should have the hang of this and feeling more confident in your calls. That first call might have felt awkward, but now that you've made four calls, how do you feel right now as you look back on that first call? Maybe you've opened lines of communication that have been shut down for some time; maybe a relationship was rekindled, and maybe both of you have a better understanding of each other. Whatever you've experienced, isn't it a remarkable feeling? It's the kind of feeling that makes you want to keep on going. I wonder who you're going to call next week…

"You define your own life. Don't let other people write your script."
Oprah Winfrey

Week 5

The person I'm acknowledging and will call this week is:

_____

I'm grateful for this person who has influenced me, and is important to me, because:

_____
_____
_____
_____
_____
_____
_____
_____
_____
_____
_____
_____
_____
_____
_____
_____
_____
_____

Reactions:

The reaction of _____ was:
(person you called)

_____
_____
_____
_____

I had the following thoughts, feelings, and emotions just before reaching this person:

_____
_____

I had the following thoughts, feelings, and emotions while I was reading the eulogy:

_____
_____
_____
_____

After saying good-bye, I have the following thoughts, feelings, and emotions:

_____
_____
_____
_____
_____

"You are never too old to set another goal or to dream a new dream."
Malala Yousafzai

Week 6

The person I'm acknowledging and will call this week is:

_____

I'm grateful for this person who has influenced me, and is important to me, because:

_____
_____
_____
_____
_____
_____
_____
_____
_____
_____
_____
_____
_____
_____
_____
_____
_____
_____
_____

Reactions:

The reaction of _____ was:
(person you called)

_____
_____
_____
_____

I had the following thoughts, feelings, and emotions just before reaching this person:

_____
_____

I had the following thoughts, feelings, and emotions while I was reading the eulogy:

_____
_____
_____
_____

After saying good-bye, I have the following thoughts, feelings, and emotions:

_____
_____
_____
_____
_____
_____

"In a gentle way, you can shake the world."
Mahatma Gandhi

Week 7

The person I'm acknowledging and will call this week is:

_____

I'm grateful for this person who has influenced me, and is important to me, because:

_____
_____
_____
_____
_____
_____
_____
_____
_____
_____
_____
_____
_____
_____
_____
_____
_____
_____

Reactions:

The reaction of _____ was:
(person you called)

_____
_____
_____
_____

I had the following thoughts, feelings, and emotions just before reaching this person:

_____
_____

I had the following thoughts, feelings, and emotions while I was reading the eulogy:

_____
_____
_____
_____

After saying good-bye, I have the following thoughts, feelings, and emotions:

_____
_____
_____
_____
_____

"Try to be a rainbow in someone's cloud."
Maya Angelou

Week 8

The person I'm acknowledging and will call this week is:

_____

I'm grateful for this person who has influenced me, and is important to me, because:

_____
_____
_____
_____
_____
_____
_____
_____
_____
_____
_____
_____
_____
_____
_____
_____
_____
_____
_____
_____

Reactions:

The reaction of _____ was:
(person you called)

_____
_____
_____
_____

I had the following thoughts, feelings, and emotions just before reaching this person:

_____
_____

I had the following thoughts, feelings, and emotions while I was reading the eulogy:

_____
_____
_____
_____

After saying good-bye, I have the following thoughts, feelings, and emotions:

_____
_____
_____
_____
_____

> *"We must let go of the life we have planned, so as to accept the one that is waiting for us."*
> Joseph Campbell

Week 9

The person I'm acknowledging and will call this week is:

_____

I'm grateful for this person who has influenced me, and is important to me, because:

_____
_____
_____
_____
_____
_____
_____
_____
_____
_____
_____
_____
_____
_____
_____
_____
_____
_____
_____
_____

Reactions:

The reaction of _____ was:
                                  (person you called)

_____
_____
_____
_____

I had the following thoughts, feelings, and emotions just before reaching this person:

_____
_____

I had the following thoughts, feelings, and emotions while I was reading the eulogy:

_____
_____
_____
_____

After saying good-bye, I have the following thoughts, feelings, and emotions:

_____
_____
_____
_____
_____

"Real change, enduring change, happens one step at a time."
Ruth Bader Ginsburg

Week 10

The person I'm acknowledging and will call this week is:

_____

I'm grateful for this person who has influenced me, and is important to me, because:

_____
_____
_____
_____
_____
_____
_____
_____
_____
_____
_____
_____
_____
_____
_____
_____
_____
_____

Reactions:

The reaction of _____ was:
(person you called)

_____
_____
_____
_____

I had the following thoughts, feelings, and emotions just before reaching this person:

_____
_____

I had the following thoughts, feelings, and emotions while I was reading the eulogy:

_____
_____
_____
_____

After saying good-bye, I have the following thoughts, feelings, and emotions:

_____
_____
_____
_____
_____

"Live your beliefs and you can turn the world around."
Henry David Thoreau

Week 11

The person I'm acknowledging and will call this week is:

_____

I'm grateful for this person who has influenced me, and is important to me, because:

_____
_____
_____
_____
_____
_____
_____
_____
_____
_____
_____
_____
_____
_____
_____
_____
_____
_____

Reactions:

The reaction of _____ was:
(person you called)

_____
_____
_____
_____

I had the following thoughts, feelings, and emotions just before reaching this person:

_____
_____

I had the following thoughts, feelings, and emotions while I was reading the eulogy:

_____
_____
_____
_____

After saying good-bye, I have the following thoughts, feelings, and emotions:

_____
_____
_____
_____
_____

*"When you've seen beyond yourself, then you may find,
peace of mind is waiting there."*
George Harrison

Week 12

The person I'm acknowledging and will call this week is:

_____

I'm grateful for this person who has influenced me, and is important to me, because:

_____
_____
_____
_____
_____
_____
_____
_____
_____
_____
_____
_____
_____
_____
_____
_____
_____
_____

Reactions:

The reaction of _____ was:
(person you called)

_____
_____
_____
_____

I had the following thoughts, feelings, and emotions just before reaching this person:

_____
_____

I had the following thoughts, feelings, and emotions while I was reading the eulogy:

_____
_____
_____
_____

After saying good-bye, I have the following thoughts, feelings, and emotions:

_____
_____
_____
_____
_____

"The power of imagination makes us infinite."
John Muir

Week 13

The person I'm acknowledging and will call this week is:

_____

I'm grateful for this person who has influenced me, and is important to me, because:

_____
_____
_____
_____
_____
_____
_____
_____
_____
_____
_____
_____
_____
_____
_____
_____
_____
_____
_____

Reactions:

The reaction of _____ was:
(person you called)

_____
_____
_____
_____

I had the following thoughts, feelings, and emotions just before reaching this person:

_____
_____

I had the following thoughts, feelings, and emotions while I was reading the eulogy:

_____
_____
_____
_____

After saying good-bye, I have the following thoughts, feelings, and emotions:

_____
_____
_____
_____
_____

"Never let the fear of striking out keep you from playing the game."
Babe Ruth

Week 14

The person I'm acknowledging and will call this week is:

_____

I'm grateful for this person who has influenced me, and is important to me, because:

_____
_____
_____
_____
_____
_____
_____
_____
_____
_____
_____
_____
_____
_____
_____
_____
_____

Reactions:

The reaction of _____ was:
(person you called)

_____
_____
_____
_____

I had the following thoughts, feelings, and emotions just before reaching this person:

_____
_____

I had the following thoughts, feelings, and emotions while I was reading the eulogy:

_____
_____
_____
_____

After saying good-bye, I have the following thoughts, feelings, and emotions:

_____
_____
_____
_____
_____

"Not how long, but how well you have lived is the main thing."
Seneca

Week 15

The person I'm acknowledging and will call this week is:

_____

I'm grateful for this person who has influenced me, and is important to me, because:

_____
_____
_____
_____
_____
_____
_____
_____
_____
_____
_____
_____
_____
_____
_____
_____
_____

Reactions:

The reaction of _____ was:
(person you called)

_____
_____
_____
_____

I had the following thoughts, feelings, and emotions just before reaching this person:

_____
_____

I had the following thoughts, feelings, and emotions while I was reading the eulogy:

_____
_____
_____
_____

After saying good-bye, I have the following thoughts, feelings, and emotions:

_____
_____
_____
_____
_____

"If life were predictable it would cease to be life, and be without flavor."
Eleanor Roosevelt

Week 16

The person I'm acknowledging and will call this week is:

_____

I'm grateful for this person who has influenced me, and is important to me, because:

_____
_____
_____
_____
_____
_____
_____
_____
_____
_____
_____
_____
_____
_____
_____
_____
_____

Reactions:

The reaction of _____ was:
(person you called)

_____
_____
_____
_____

I had the following thoughts, feelings, and emotions just before reaching this person:

_____
_____

I had the following thoughts, feelings, and emotions while I was reading the eulogy:

_____
_____
_____
_____

After saying good-bye, I have the following thoughts, feelings, and emotions:

_____
_____
_____
_____
_____

"Life is not a problem to be solved, but a reality to be experienced."
Soren Kierkegaard

Week 17

The person I'm acknowledging and will call this week is:

_____

I'm grateful for this person who has influenced me, and is important to me, because:

_____
_____
_____
_____
_____
_____
_____
_____
_____
_____
_____
_____
_____
_____
_____
_____
_____
_____
_____

Reactions:

The reaction of _____ was:
(person you called)

_____
_____
_____
_____

I had the following thoughts, feelings, and emotions just before reaching this person:

_____
_____

I had the following thoughts, feelings, and emotions while I was reading the eulogy:

_____
_____
_____
_____

After saying good-bye, I have the following thoughts, feelings, and emotions:

_____
_____
_____
_____
_____

"Don't settle for what life gives you; make life better and build something."
Ashton Kutcher

Week 18

The person I'm acknowledging and will call this week is:

_____

I'm grateful for this person who has influenced me, and is important to me, because:

_____
_____
_____
_____
_____
_____
_____
_____
_____
_____
_____
_____
_____
_____
_____
_____
_____
_____
_____

Reactions:

The reaction of _____ was:
(person you called)

_____
_____
_____
_____

I had the following thoughts, feelings, and emotions just before reaching this person:

_____
_____

I had the following thoughts, feelings, and emotions while I was reading the eulogy:

_____
_____
_____
_____

After saying good-bye, I have the following thoughts, feelings, and emotions:

_____
_____
_____
_____
_____

> *"Live for each second without hesitation."*
> Elton John

Week 19

The person I'm acknowledging and will call this week is:

_____

I'm grateful for this person who has influenced me, and is important to me, because:

_____
_____
_____
_____
_____
_____
_____
_____
_____
_____
_____
_____
_____
_____
_____
_____
_____
_____
_____
_____

Reactions:

The reaction of _____ was:
(person you called)

_____
_____
_____
_____

I had the following thoughts, feelings, and emotions just before reaching this person:

_____
_____

I had the following thoughts, feelings, and emotions while I was reading the eulogy:

_____
_____
_____
_____

After saying good-bye, I have the following thoughts, feelings, and emotions:

_____
_____
_____
_____
_____

"The healthiest response to life is joy."
Deepak Chopra

Week 20

The person I'm acknowledging and will call this week is:

_____

I'm grateful for this person who has influenced me, and is important to me, because:

_____
_____
_____
_____
_____
_____
_____
_____
_____
_____
_____
_____
_____
_____
_____
_____
_____
_____
_____

Reactions:

The reaction of _____ was:
(person you called)

_____
_____
_____
_____

I had the following thoughts, feelings, and emotions just before reaching this person:

_____
_____

I had the following thoughts, feelings, and emotions while I was reading the eulogy:

_____
_____
_____
_____

After saying good-bye, I have the following thoughts, feelings, and emotions:

_____
_____
_____
_____
_____
_____

"In three words, I can sum up everything I've learned about life: It goes on."
Robert Frost

Week 21

The person I'm acknowledging and will call this week is:

_____

I'm grateful for this person who has influenced me, and is important to me, because:

_____
_____
_____
_____
_____
_____
_____
_____
_____
_____
_____
_____
_____
_____
_____
_____
_____
_____
_____
_____

Reactions:

The reaction of _____ was:
(person you called)

_____
_____
_____
_____

I had the following thoughts, feelings, and emotions just before reaching this person:

_____
_____

I had the following thoughts, feelings, and emotions while I was reading the eulogy:

_____
_____
_____
_____

After saying good-bye, I have the following thoughts, feelings, and emotions:

_____
_____
_____
_____
_____
_____

"Life is a flower of which love is the honey."
Victor Hugo

Week 22

The person I'm acknowledging and will call this week is:
_____

I'm grateful for this person who has influenced me, and is important to me, because:

_____
_____
_____
_____
_____
_____
_____
_____
_____
_____
_____
_____
_____
_____
_____
_____
_____
_____

Reactions:

The reaction of _____ was:
                            (person you called)

_____
_____
_____

I had the following thoughts, feelings, and emotions just before reaching this person:

_____
_____

I had the following thoughts, feelings, and emotions while I was reading the eulogy:

_____
_____
_____
_____

After saying good-bye, I have the following thoughts, feelings, and emotions:

_____
_____
_____
_____
_____

"Keep smiling, because life is a beautiful thing and there's so much to smile about."
Marilyn Monroe

Week 23

The person I'm acknowledging and will call this week is:

_____

I'm grateful for this person who has influenced me, and is important to me, because:

_____
_____
_____
_____
_____
_____
_____
_____
_____
_____
_____
_____
_____
_____
_____
_____
_____

Reactions:

The reaction of _____ was:
(person you called)

_____
_____
_____
_____

I had the following thoughts, feelings, and emotions just before reaching this person:

_____
_____

I had the following thoughts, feelings, and emotions while I was reading the eulogy:

_____
_____
_____
_____

After saying good-bye, I have the following thoughts, feelings, and emotions:

_____
_____
_____
_____

"Life is about making an impact, not making an income."
Kevin Kruse

Week 24

The person I'm acknowledging and will call this week is:

_____

I'm grateful for this person who has influenced me, and is important to me, because:

_____
_____
_____
_____
_____
_____
_____
_____
_____
_____
_____
_____
_____
_____
_____
_____
_____

Reactions:

The reaction of _____ was:
(person you called)

_____
_____
_____
_____

I had the following thoughts, feelings, and emotions just before reaching this person:

_____
_____

I had the following thoughts, feelings, and emotions while I was reading the eulogy:

_____
_____
_____
_____

After saying good-bye, I have the following thoughts, feelings, and emotions:

_____
_____
_____
_____

"It is our choices that show what we truly are, far more than our abilities."
J. K. Rowling

Week 25

The person I'm acknowledging and will call this week is:

_____

I'm grateful for this person who has influenced me, and is important to me, because:

_____
_____
_____
_____
_____
_____
_____
_____
_____
_____
_____
_____
_____
_____
_____
_____
_____

Reactions:

The reaction of _____ was:
(person you called)

_____
_____
_____
_____

I had the following thoughts, feelings, and emotions just before reaching this person:

_____
_____

I had the following thoughts, feelings, and emotions while I was reading the eulogy:

_____
_____
_____
_____

After saying good-bye, I have the following thoughts, feelings, and emotions:

_____
_____
_____
_____
_____

"All life is an experiment. The more experiments you make, the better."
Ralph Waldo Emerson

Week 26

The person I'm acknowledging and will call this week is:

_____

I'm grateful for this person who has influenced me, and is important to me, because:

_____
_____
_____
_____
_____
_____
_____
_____
_____
_____
_____
_____
_____
_____
_____
_____
_____
_____
_____
_____

Reactions:

The reaction of _____ was:
(person you called)

_____
_____
_____
_____

I had the following thoughts, feelings, and emotions just before reaching this person:

_____
_____

I had the following thoughts, feelings, and emotions while I was reading the eulogy:

_____
_____
_____
_____

After saying good-bye, I have the following thoughts, feelings, and emotions:

_____
_____
_____
_____
_____

Progress Check 2

Another check in, You're halfway through your living eulogies now. Maybe this is a good time for some personal reflection.

Think about that first week, think about your thoughts and feelings about that first call. What's different now? What has changed in you in the way you interact with the world around you? What kind of changes have you noticed about your own happiness and the way you cope with difficulties in your life? Has anyone said anything to you about your outlook on life or your attitude? Have there been any comments about you from your family, friends, or co-workers?

In doing these living eulogies for a half a year now, think of the number of people you've influenced. Remember those first four people and how you sharing your gratitude was multiplied exponentially, and there were people you never met who were affected by those first four calls. Each of those four actions created a chain-reaction of kindness and gratitude.

Most people spend about five minutes writing a eulogy and then spend another five minutes or so on the phone reading that eulogy. That's a total of 10 minutes a week. An investment of just 10 minutes of your time each week did more good than you'll ever know. In the time it would take you to listen to three songs on your favorite wireless streaming device, you changed the world for someone each week for the last 26 weeks. And the world changed for that person had a domino effect that, at this point, is impossible to measure. That's the power of sharing gratitude.

Like a snowball that began by slowly rolling down a hill at first, your actions have now grown in size and speed. In fact, your actions are now becoming an avalanche of goodness and kindness flowing through you and all around you. You are unstoppable! And, it feels good, doesn't it? As good as you feel, think of how those 26 people feel; how it felt for them to hear your words. And, according to studies, you are happier for sharing your gratitude, and the people you called have had the opportunity to hear not just that you're grateful for them, but they heard why you're grateful for them in your life.

Now, it's time for the second half of your living eulogies. Enjoy the journey!

"In the long run, the sharpest weapon of all is a kind and gentle spirit."
Anne Frank

Week 27

The person I'm acknowledging and will call this week is:

_____

I'm grateful for this person who has influenced me, and is important to me, because:

_____
_____
_____
_____
_____
_____
_____
_____
_____
_____
_____
_____
_____
_____
_____
_____
_____
_____
_____
_____

Reactions:

The reaction of _____ was:
                     (person you called)

_____

_____

_____

_____

I had the following thoughts, feelings, and emotions just before reaching this person:

_____

_____

I had the following thoughts, feelings, and emotions while I was reading the eulogy:

_____

_____

_____

_____

After saying good-bye, I have the following thoughts, feelings, and emotions:

_____

_____

_____

_____

_____

"Your image isn't your character. Character is what you are as a person."
Derek Jeter

Week 28

The person I'm acknowledging and will call this week is:

_____

I'm grateful for this person who has influenced me, and is important to me, because:

_____
_____
_____
_____
_____
_____
_____
_____
_____
_____
_____
_____
_____
_____
_____
_____
_____
_____
_____
_____

Reactions:

The reaction of _____ was:
                                (person you called)

_____
_____
_____
_____

I had the following thoughts, feelings, and emotions just before reaching this person:

_____
_____

I had the following thoughts, feelings, and emotions while I was reading the eulogy:

_____
_____
_____
_____

After saying good-bye, I have the following thoughts, feelings, and emotions:

_____
_____
_____
_____
_____

"I believe that nothing in life is unimportant; every moment can be a beginning."
John McLeod

Week 29

The person I'm acknowledging and will call this week is:

_____

I'm grateful for this person who has influenced me, and is important to me, because:

_____
_____
_____
_____
_____
_____
_____
_____
_____
_____
_____
_____
_____
_____
_____
_____
_____
_____
_____

Reactions:

The reaction of _____ was:
(person you called)

_____
_____
_____
_____

I had the following thoughts, feelings, and emotions just before reaching this person:

_____
_____

I had the following thoughts, feelings, and emotions while I was reading the eulogy:

_____
_____
_____
_____

After saying good-bye, I have the following thoughts, feelings, and emotions:

_____
_____
_____
_____
_____

"If we don't change, we don't grow. If we don't grow, we aren't really living."
Gail Sheehy

Week 30

The person I'm acknowledging and will call this week is:

_____

I'm grateful for this person who has influenced me, and is important to me, because:

_____
_____
_____
_____
_____
_____
_____
_____
_____
_____
_____
_____
_____
_____
_____
_____
_____

Reactions:

The reaction of _____ was:
                       (person you called)

_____
_____
_____

I had the following thoughts, feelings, and emotions just before reaching this person:

_____
_____

I had the following thoughts, feelings, and emotions while I was reading the eulogy:

_____
_____
_____

After saying good-bye, I have the following thoughts, feelings, and emotions:

_____
_____
_____
_____

"Life doesn't require that we be the best, only that we try our best."
H. Jackson Brown Jr.

Week 31

The person I'm acknowledging and will call this week is:

_____

I'm grateful for this person who has influenced me, and is important to me, because:

_____
_____
_____
_____
_____
_____
_____
_____
_____
_____
_____
_____
_____
_____
_____
_____
_____
_____
_____

Reactions:

The reaction of _____ was:
                                (person you called)

_____
_____
_____
_____

I had the following thoughts, feelings, and emotions just before reaching this person:

_____
_____

I had the following thoughts, feelings, and emotions while I was reading the eulogy:

_____
_____
_____
_____

After saying good-bye, I have the following thoughts, feelings, and emotions:

_____
_____
_____
_____
_____

> *"Life isn't about waiting for the storm to pass, it's about learning to dance in the rain."*
> Vivian Greene

Week 32

The person I'm acknowledging and will call this week is:

_____

I'm grateful for this person who has influenced me, and is important to me, because:

_____
_____
_____
_____
_____
_____
_____
_____
_____
_____
_____
_____
_____
_____
_____
_____
_____

Reactions:

The reaction of _____ was:
(person you called)

_____
_____
_____
_____

I had the following thoughts, feelings, and emotions just before reaching this person:

_____
_____

I had the following thoughts, feelings, and emotions while I was reading the eulogy:

_____
_____
_____
_____

After saying good-bye, I have the following thoughts, feelings, and emotions:

_____
_____
_____
_____
_____

"You can't put a limit on anything. The more you dream, the farther you get."
Michael Phelps

Week 33

The person I'm acknowledging and will call this week is:

_____

I'm grateful for this person who has influenced me, and is important to me, because:

_____
_____
_____
_____
_____
_____
_____
_____
_____
_____
_____
_____
_____
_____
_____
_____
_____
_____

Reactions:

The reaction of _____ was:
(person you called)

_____
_____
_____
_____

I had the following thoughts, feelings, and emotions just before reaching this person:

_____
_____

I had the following thoughts, feelings, and emotions while I was reading the eulogy:

_____
_____
_____
_____

After saying good-bye, I have the following thoughts, feelings, and emotions:

_____
_____
_____
_____
_____

"There is strength in the differences between us; there is comfort where we overlap."
Ani DiFranco

Week 34

The person I'm acknowledging and will call this week is:

_____

I'm grateful for this person who has influenced me, and is important to me, because:

_____
_____
_____
_____
_____
_____
_____
_____
_____
_____
_____
_____
_____
_____
_____
_____
_____
_____
_____

Reactions:

The reaction of _____ was:
(person you called)

_____
_____
_____
_____

I had the following thoughts, feelings, and emotions just before reaching this person:

_____
_____

I had the following thoughts, feelings, and emotions while I was reading the eulogy:

_____
_____
_____
_____

After saying good-bye, I have the following thoughts, feelings, and emotions:

_____
_____
_____
_____

"There are no passengers on spaceship earth. We are all crew."
Marshall McLuhan

Week 35

The person I'm acknowledging and will call this week is:

_____

I'm grateful for this person who has influenced me, and is important to me, because:

_____
_____
_____
_____
_____
_____
_____
_____
_____
_____
_____
_____
_____
_____
_____
_____
_____

Reactions:

The reaction of _____ was:
(person you called)

_____
_____
_____
_____

I had the following thoughts, feelings, and emotions just before reaching this person:

_____
_____

I had the following thoughts, feelings, and emotions while I was reading the eulogy:

_____
_____
_____
_____

After saying good-bye, I have the following thoughts, feelings, and emotions:

_____
_____
_____
_____
_____

"You can't move forward if you're still hanging on."
Sue Fitzmaurice

Week 36

The person I'm acknowledging and will call this week is:

_____

I'm grateful for this person who has influenced me, and is important to me, because:

_____
_____
_____
_____
_____
_____
_____
_____
_____
_____
_____
_____
_____
_____
_____
_____
_____
_____

Reactions:

The reaction of _____ was:
(person you called)

_____
_____
_____
_____

I had the following thoughts, feelings, and emotions just before reaching this person:

_____
_____

I had the following thoughts, feelings, and emotions while I was reading the eulogy:

_____
_____
_____
_____

After saying good-bye, I have the following thoughts, feelings, and emotions:

_____
_____
_____
_____

"Be sure to put your feet in the right place, then stand firm."
Abraham Lincoln

Week 37

The person I'm acknowledging and will call this week is:

_____

I'm grateful for this person who has influenced me, and is important to me, because:

_____
_____
_____
_____
_____
_____
_____
_____
_____
_____
_____
_____
_____
_____
_____
_____

Reactions:

The reaction of _____ was:
(person you called)

_____
_____
_____
_____

I had the following thoughts, feelings, and emotions just before reaching this person:

_____
_____

I had the following thoughts, feelings, and emotions while I was reading the eulogy:

_____
_____
_____
_____

After saying good-bye, I have the following thoughts, feelings, and emotions:

_____
_____
_____
_____
_____

"Don't be afraid to give up the good to go for the great."
John D. Rockefeller

Week 38

The person I'm acknowledging and will call this week is:

_____

I'm grateful for this person who has influenced me, and is important to me, because:

_____
_____
_____
_____
_____
_____
_____
_____
_____
_____
_____
_____
_____
_____
_____
_____
_____
_____
_____
_____

Reactions:

The reaction of _____ was:
(person you called)

_____
_____
_____
_____

I had the following thoughts, feelings, and emotions just before reaching this person:

_____
_____

I had the following thoughts, feelings, and emotions while I was reading the eulogy:

_____
_____
_____
_____

After saying good-bye, I have the following thoughts, feelings, and emotions:

_____
_____
_____
_____

"You only live once, but if you do it right, once is enough."
Mae West

Week 39

The person I'm acknowledging and will call this week is:

_____

I'm grateful for this person who has influenced me, and is important to me, because:

_____
_____
_____
_____
_____
_____
_____
_____
_____
_____
_____
_____
_____
_____
_____
_____
_____
_____

Reactions:

The reaction of _____ was:
                (person you called)

_____
_____
_____
_____

I had the following thoughts, feelings, and emotions just before reaching this person:

_____
_____

I had the following thoughts, feelings, and emotions while I was reading the eulogy:

_____
_____
_____
_____

After saying good-bye, I have the following thoughts, feelings, and emotions:

_____
_____
_____
_____
_____

"Life is available only in the present."
Thich Nhat Hanh

Week 40

The person I'm acknowledging and will call this week is:

_____

I'm grateful for this person who has influenced me, and is important to me, because:

_____
_____
_____
_____
_____
_____
_____
_____
_____
_____
_____
_____
_____
_____
_____
_____
_____

Reactions:

The reaction of _____ was:
(person you called)

_____
_____
_____
_____

I had the following thoughts, feelings, and emotions just before reaching this person:

_____
_____

I had the following thoughts, feelings, and emotions while I was reading the eulogy:

_____
_____
_____
_____

After saying good-bye, I have the following thoughts, feelings, and emotions:

_____
_____
_____
_____
_____

"Courage is the power to let go of the familiar."
Raymond Lindquist

Week 41

The person I'm acknowledging and will call this week is:

_____

I'm grateful for this person who has influenced me, and is important to me, because:

_____
_____
_____
_____
_____
_____
_____
_____
_____
_____
_____
_____
_____
_____
_____
_____
_____

Reactions:

The reaction of _____ was:
(person you called)

_____
_____
_____
_____

I had the following thoughts, feelings, and emotions just before reaching this person:

_____
_____

I had the following thoughts, feelings, and emotions while I was reading the eulogy:

_____
_____
_____
_____

After saying good-bye, I have the following thoughts, feelings, and emotions:

_____
_____
_____
_____
_____

"Take chances, make mistakes. That's how you grow."
Mary Tyler Moore

Week 42

The person I'm acknowledging and will call this week is:

_____

I'm grateful for this person who has influenced me, and is important to me, because:

_____
_____
_____
_____
_____
_____
_____
_____
_____
_____
_____
_____
_____
_____
_____
_____
_____
_____

Reactions:

The reaction of _____ was:
(person you called)

_____
_____
_____
_____

I had the following thoughts, feelings, and emotions just before reaching this person:

_____
_____

I had the following thoughts, feelings, and emotions while I was reading the eulogy:

_____
_____
_____
_____

After saying good-bye, I have the following thoughts, feelings, and emotions:

_____
_____
_____
_____

"Every burden is a blessing."
Walt Kelly

Week 43

The person I'm acknowledging and will call this week is:

_____

I'm grateful for this person who has influenced me, and is important to me, because:

_____
_____
_____
_____
_____
_____
_____
_____
_____
_____
_____
_____
_____
_____
_____
_____
_____
_____
_____
_____

Reactions:

The reaction of _____ was:
               (person you called)

_____
_____
_____
_____

I had the following thoughts, feelings, and emotions just before reaching this person:

_____
_____

I had the following thoughts, feelings, and emotions while I was reading the eulogy:

_____
_____
_____
_____

After saying good-bye, I have the following thoughts, feelings, and emotions:

_____
_____
_____
_____
_____

"Change the way you look at things, and the things you look at change."
Wayne W. Dyer

Week 44

The person I'm acknowledging and will call this week is:

_____

I'm grateful for this person who has influenced me, and is important to me, because:

_____
_____
_____
_____
_____
_____
_____
_____
_____
_____
_____
_____
_____
_____
_____
_____
_____
_____
_____
_____

Reactions:

The reaction of _____ was:
(person you called)

_____
_____
_____
_____

I had the following thoughts, feelings, and emotions just before reaching this person:

_____
_____

I had the following thoughts, feelings, and emotions while I was reading the eulogy:

_____
_____
_____
_____

After saying good-bye, I have the following thoughts, feelings, and emotions:

_____
_____
_____
_____
_____

"Freedom comes from strength and self-reliance."
Lisa Murkowski

Week 45

The person I'm acknowledging and will call this week is:

_____

I'm grateful for this person who has influenced me, and is important to me, because:

_____
_____
_____
_____
_____
_____
_____
_____
_____
_____
_____
_____
_____
_____
_____
_____

Reactions:

The reaction of _____ was:
(person you called)

_____
_____
_____
_____

I had the following thoughts, feelings, and emotions just before reaching this person:

_____
_____

I had the following thoughts, feelings, and emotions while I was reading the eulogy:

_____
_____
_____
_____

After saying good-bye, I have the following thoughts, feelings, and emotions:

_____
_____
_____
_____

"Be like a tree and let the dead leaves drop."
Rumi

Week 46

The person I'm acknowledging and will call this week is:

_____

I'm grateful for this person who has influenced me, and is important to me, because:

_____
_____
_____
_____
_____
_____
_____
_____
_____
_____
_____
_____
_____
_____
_____
_____
_____
_____

Reactions:

The reaction of _____ was:
                (person you called)

_____
_____
_____
_____

I had the following thoughts, feelings, and emotions just before reaching this person:

_____
_____

I had the following thoughts, feelings, and emotions while I was reading the eulogy:

_____
_____
_____
_____

After saying good-bye, I have the following thoughts, feelings, and emotions:

_____
_____
_____
_____
_____

"Life is 10 percent what you make it, and 90 percent how you take it."
Irving Berlin

Week 47

The person I'm acknowledging and will call this week is:

_____

I'm grateful for this person who has influenced me, and is important to me, because:

_____
_____
_____
_____
_____
_____
_____
_____
_____
_____
_____
_____
_____
_____
_____
_____
_____

Reactions:

The reaction of _____ was:
(person you called)

_____
_____
_____
_____

I had the following thoughts, feelings, and emotions just before reaching this person:

_____
_____

I had the following thoughts, feelings, and emotions while I was reading the eulogy:

_____
_____
_____
_____

After saying good-bye, I have the following thoughts, feelings, and emotions:

_____
_____
_____
_____
_____

"Forgive yourself for your faults and your mistakes and move on."
Les Brown

Week 48

The person I'm acknowledging and will call this week is:

_____

I'm grateful for this person who has influenced me, and is important to me, because:

_____
_____
_____
_____
_____
_____
_____
_____
_____
_____
_____
_____
_____
_____
_____
_____
_____
_____
_____
_____

Reactions:

The reaction of _____ was:
(person you called)

_____
_____
_____
_____

I had the following thoughts, feelings, and emotions just before reaching this person:

_____
_____

I had the following thoughts, feelings, and emotions while I was reading the eulogy:

_____
_____
_____
_____

After saying good-bye, I have the following thoughts, feelings, and emotions:

_____
_____
_____
_____
_____

Progress Check 3

One final check in as you're at the last month of your journal, the last four people to share their living eulogies with. Did the last 11 months go by slow or did they seem to go by fast? Most people say the days seem to go by slow, but the months seem to fly by.

How have the responses been for the most part? Surely there are eulogies that you remember easily, and you've had responses that were heartwarming. And, you've probably had a response or two that were less than what you hoped for. And, that's ok. You shared something very personal, and very special, with someone who had a positive influence in your life. And, by doing so, you opened a door for each one of them. Whether they took the invitation to enter through the door was up to them, and their response says nothing about you. Remember, your reason for sharing a living eulogy was to let those people who are important in your life know what they mean to you. What they do with that information is up to them.

But, also remember the science behind sharing gratitude. You've changed yourself, and your actions changed the lives of no less than 48 people. And, those 48 people went on and changed countless lives in the weeks and months since you called them. It started with that first call, and it's kept going because of your commitment to kindness and happiness; it's kept going because you want to make sure certain people in your life know what they mean to you. What a gift you've given them!

I would suggest to you that these next four weeks are going to go by fast, and you might even regret that this is coming to an end. Here's an idea: Stay in the moment, and each week focus on that person on your list. Allow yourself to be fully present in each week and not thinking about the future weeks; let each of the next four weeks come at their own pace. In doing so, you'll be able to offer your honest interaction with each person as each week comes and goes. After all, don't they deserve it as much as the other people that you called in the previous months?

With that in mind, enjoy the next four weeks, share your gift of gratitude, and don't rush anything (or regret anything). Be in the moment and be in each moment of the moment, and you'll find these upcoming calls will be very special. You deserve it. And these next four people on your list deserve it. We'll talk again after you've completed your 52nd call.

"There are far better things ahead than any we leave behind."
C.S. Lewis

Week 49

The person I'm acknowledging and will call this week is:

_____

I'm grateful for this person who has influenced me, and is important to me, because:

_____
_____
_____
_____
_____
_____
_____
_____
_____
_____
_____
_____
_____
_____
_____
_____
_____

Reactions:

The reaction of _____ was:
(person you called)

_____
_____
_____
_____

I had the following thoughts, feelings, and emotions just before reaching this person:

_____
_____

I had the following thoughts, feelings, and emotions while I was reading the eulogy:

_____
_____
_____
_____

After saying good-bye, I have the following thoughts, feelings, and emotions:

_____
_____
_____
_____
_____

"Continual effort, not strength or intelligence, is the key to unlocking our potential"
Liane Cordes

Week 50

The person I'm acknowledging and will call this week is:

_____

I'm grateful for this person who has influenced me, and is important to me, because:

_____
_____
_____
_____
_____
_____
_____
_____
_____
_____
_____
_____
_____
_____
_____
_____
_____
_____

Reactions:

The reaction of _____ was:
(person you called)

_____
_____
_____
_____

I had the following thoughts, feelings, and emotions just before reaching this person:

_____
_____

I had the following thoughts, feelings, and emotions while I was reading the eulogy:

_____
_____
_____
_____

After saying good-bye, I have the following thoughts, feelings, and emotions:

_____
_____
_____
_____
_____

"All things are difficult before they are easy."
Thomas Fuller

Week 51

The person I'm acknowledging and will call this week is:

_____

I'm grateful for this person who has influenced me, and is important to me, because:

_____
_____
_____
_____
_____
_____
_____
_____
_____
_____
_____
_____
_____
_____
_____
_____
_____

Reactions:

The reaction of _____ was:
(person you called)

_____
_____
_____
_____

I had the following thoughts, feelings, and emotions just before reaching this person:

_____
_____

I had the following thoughts, feelings, and emotions while I was reading the eulogy:

_____
_____
_____
_____

After saying good-bye, I have the following thoughts, feelings, and emotions:

_____
_____
_____
_____

"Good actions give strength to ourselves and inspire good actions in others."
Plato

Week 52

The person I'm acknowledging and will call this week is:

_____

I'm grateful for this person who has influenced me, and is important to me, because:

_____
_____
_____
_____
_____
_____
_____
_____
_____
_____
_____
_____
_____
_____
_____
_____
_____

Reactions:

The reaction of _____ was:
(person you called)

_____
_____
_____
_____

I had the following thoughts, feelings, and emotions just before reaching this person:

_____
_____

I had the following thoughts, feelings, and emotions while I was reading the eulogy:

_____
_____
_____
_____

After saying good-bye, I have the following thoughts, feelings, and emotions:

_____
_____
_____
_____
_____

The Living Eulogy Journal
A Year of Sharing Gratitude and Becoming Happier

Section 3

Chapter 5: Taking It To Another Level

How does it feel now that a full year has passed? How have the past 52 weeks been different than previous years? What's changed in the relationships of those you wrote about? What's changed in you?

Do you realize how you've changed your brain chemistry? Your brain has slowly been re-wired over the past 12 months to find words that describe gratitude for others. And, in doing so, the feel-good hormones have been released when you shared your eulogies and when you received feedback from those very special people in your life. In fact, just knowing that your words changed the lives of others has caused your brain to release some of those feel-good hormones. In essence, you have trained your brain so that you feel better about life; you feel happier and you experience more joy in your life.

And, the good news is, you don't have to stop here! Many people, after they get the hang of writing their gratitude for others, buy a simple notebook and continue sharing their living eulogies – using simple lined notebooks. Of course, I would love it if you bought another *Living Eulogy Journal* and started over with another 52 weeks of new people you've met; but the truth is, you now have the tools inside you to do it yourself. Just thinking about the past year, I bet you can think of dozens of people who weren't on your original list that you would like to share your gratitude with. Why stop now?

You've forever changed the lives of 52 people this past year; people who, before you called them, didn't know the depth of your gratitude or perhaps knew you were grateful, but didn't know why. Their lives have been changed for the better because of you. And, what about the lives that have been touched by those 52 people? Think for a minute about how any one of those 52 people felt a little better after you called them and how they might have treated another person because of it. This is the power of gratitude. People you don't know, and will probably never meet, will have had their lives changed because of your simple act of kindness – your sharing of your gratitude with someone special in your life.

So, again: Why stop now?

While you consider some of the things offered here, are you willing to take this level of gratitude to the next level? Are you up for a challenge? Sure, you are!

The next section offers you opportunities to share gratitude in a very unique way. The eulogy page that follows this is a living eulogy for… it's a living eulogy for *you*. It's very similar to the previous 52 weeks, but in this case, you won't be calling anyone after you write it.

This is a powerful tool for a roadmap on how you want to live the rest of your life – where you see your life's journey heading. It's as simple as this: Write down what you would want said about you if it was your service. It's in two parts: The first part is your eulogy up until this moment in time, up until today. The second part is your eulogy how you are going to live the rest of your life – what you envision yourself being and doing. How would someone describe you up until today, and how would someone describe the you that you want to be from now until your death.

Don't' be shy. This is your chance to write your legacy. And after you write it, you'll have the rest of your life to live it. That's the power in this eulogy – part of it has already been lived, and another part has yet to be lived. Regardless of your age or your health, today is the best day to do this. You should know that I'm over 60 years old, living with a tumor growing in my spinal cord. Most of my life is in the rearview mirror, but that doesn't mean I don't have time left to write the rest of my life. And, a living eulogy is a great (and powerful) way to do that!

So, what do you say? Isn't today the best day to get started? Great, I knew you'd say that!

The last eulogy in this journal you're holding is a very special one. It's called *The Eulogy I Never Gave*. It's your time to write a eulogy for someone who has died and you didn't get the opportunity to share your thoughts at the service. Maybe it's a family member, a loved one, a friend or a colleague. I know there are many people in my life who have died and I never had the chance to speak about how much they meant to me. Starting with my parents who died within a year of each other when I was in my early twenties, and then to a friend who died from a surgery complication, to a colleague who died from cancer. Like you, I have many regrets, and many of them are things I wish I said, but never had the opportunity. This is your chance to share your thoughts… thoughts that have been inside you for so long.

You should know that like the eulogy to yourself, this is a very powerful exercise and it can be emotional. And, now you know that it's healthy to share your emotions – to let them out unapologetically. Writing those words you always wanted to say, and then reading them out loud, helps with healing and it helps with grief.

It's up to you whether you want to complete it. And it's up to you to decide when you want to do so. There is no time frame. If, and when the time feels right, you'll know it. Think of it as a resource that's available to you if you feel you need it.

"Our lives are stories in which we write, direct and star in the leading role. Some chapters are happy while others bring lessons to learn, but we always have the power to be the heroes of our own adventures."
Joelle Speranza

Personal Eulogy: Part 1

Your name: _____

What would be said about your life up until today:

_____
_____
_____
_____
_____
_____
_____
_____
_____
_____
_____
_____
_____
_____
_____
_____
_____

Personal Eulogy: Part 2

What would be said about your life from today until your death:

The Eulogy I Never Gave

Loved one's name: _____

Your thoughts about your loved one; how you remember them:

_____
_____
_____
_____
_____
_____
_____
_____
_____
_____
_____
_____
_____
_____
_____
_____
_____
_____
_____
_____
_____

The Living Eulogy Journal

A Year of Sharing Gratitude and Becoming Happier

Section 3

Chapter 6: Closing Thoughts

If you've completed this journal, and gotten to this page, it will have been more than a year since you purchased it. As I'm sitting here writing this sentence, I can't help but to wonder what the past year has been like for you. I hope it was filled with joy and happiness; but I'm a realist as much as I am an optimist, so I understand there were probably some difficult times as well. I wonder how you coped with those times as much as I think about how you searched for reasons to be grateful for so many things in your life. And, I hope this journal had some role in your happiness, your joy, and especially your gratitude.

Two years after my father died, my oldest son was born. My father died on Thanksgiving morning in 1986, and my son was born in November of 1988. I remember one night working the midnight shift. I was a police officer, and in the early morning hours of a Monday (late Sunday night, depending how you look at it) I was driving around my sector. It was the Sunday night after Christmas, the roads were deserted, and I was doing my best to stay focused (and stay awake!). The only thing keeping me going were the songs playing on the radio.

After a familiar song finished playing, the disc jockey came on and said the next song was a new release from Mike Rutherford, the former guitarist of the band, Genesis. Rutherford had formed a new band, Mike + the Mechanics, and they just released a new album; the song was from that album. The lyrics hit me so hard I had to pull to the side of the road, put my patrol car in park, and sit there. I wept, nonstop, listening to this song play – it was as if Rutherford was singing to me. The name of the song is *The Living Years*, and it's all about the importance of telling others how we feel about them while they're still alive to hear it – in the living years.

Please, for you, and for them, share your gratitude in the living years.

If this journal, and especially the work you put into it, has made a difference in your life, I would love to hear about it. Please visit: LivingEulogyProject.org

Also feel free to become a member of our Facebook group, The Living Eulogy Project:

https://www.facebook.com/groups/1063705311106332

Made in United States
North Haven, CT
27 November 2021